For Jim,
A true poet

I'm taking pen to paper

I'm taking pen to paper
In a bid to save the world,
They'll read my fantastic prose
And hang on every word.

They'll cite me in Parliament,
And quote me on the Wiki,
And put up a big statue
Of me thinking, in the city.

I will write into the paper
And tell it as it is.
I'll mansplain the symbiosis
Between the poor and the rich.

I'll study the scrolls of Twitter,
How left and right flow and ebb,
And how when a horrible bastard dies,
They cry "Don't speak ill of the dead".

And then I'll make the dinner,
After the washing up.
I think I set myself up to fail,
As I rest in the evening, with my cup.

Let's Call A Spade A Spade

Let's call a spade a spade
Ok, a spade is a spade
But is it a metal spade
Or is it a child's beach spade?

This spade of your's
How does it fit in with your bias?
Or are you a card shark
Having a moment of pious?

What is the unpalatable fact
That has you calling this spade
I have a feeling it's your opinion
That leads you to call pomp to aid.

Next you'll be devil's advocate
Just to irritate
When it's proved a spade is not a spade
The object of the argument, now is to frustrate

The simplest salient point
If a point you cannot evade
Is that you aren't saying anything
By calling a spade a spade

Why Do We Need To Be Told How To Think?

I asked a question
Well really it was a muse
About those who moan
But really are of no use

I put it out in public
To see just how much we care
An hour later I checked
Yes, nobody was there

The philosophy of broadcasting
Is a theory of populism
Tis far easier to drum up hate
Than form a consensus decision

Debate is loud when shallow
Those are not my words
And to see venom spewing
Brings joy in controlling herds

Confining people to corners
Soccer, Twitter, Celebrities
Will keep the world's resources
In off-shore tax-free entities

It's so base and so simple
And in front of everyone's face
But I'll just log on to Social
And see the latest disgrace

Pseudo Boss

The definition of micromanagement
is the management or control
with excessive attention to minor detail.

And it takes a certain type of person
to decide they should decide
what your working life should entail.

If, for example say,
you found an easy way for something
to do a certain thing?

The role of your micromanager
is to take that certain something
and make them feel like a king.

But the micromanager usually isn't
your boss or your superior
They're usually an equate.

And while they are sitting pretty
They like to think
you think they're a mate.

If you feel you are assertive,
and boundaries aren't you
and you really like to manage,

You should join the union of micromanagers,
rain on parades
and afflict mental damage.

It's not deja vu

It's not deja vu but it is familiar
When the cuckoo brays in a damp summer arbour
A softness rests on your heart
With a sadness for the sun

Midges will spatter you in the face
A hundred kamikaze death wishes
Of this world for an hour
Before their souls vanish

It's almost as if you're cheating
Denying nature by not being cold
But she does not care of this invincibility
For the cuckoo does not let up

And there is a pervading sense of hope
That if not today then tomorrow
The true summer sun will cast
And the cars will bray instead

Not that you are hoping for fumes
But instinct tells you so
Soft day, thank god, they say
Are words, only now, I know

Dreams

It's a big cruel world out there son,
It will crush all your dreams.
But why is it like that Da?
Because everyone just wants things!

But mum says the world's your oyster!
Have you ever eaten oysters son?
Ok you might get a pearl,
An object to belong to someone.

So what are your dreams Da?
Lots son, lots son, more than a few!
So why do you keep on dreaming,
If none of them come true?

I don't know the answer son!
If I did, I would surely help,
I suppose we need to dream,
Because we believe in ourselves.

A poem about homelessness

Fuck!
It's horrible!
It's really shit!
You wouldn't like it....

A Place On Our Timeline
(For Jen)

Long into this Sunday night
On a day of mixed emotion
Vying for my attention
Exists months of aged pain

Day in and day out
Overbearing nervous ache
Engulfs my every step
Such that joy is a welcome refrain

No easier than my struggle is
The fight that's brought to you
As far as struggles go
Someone up there is turning the screw

Knowing what we bring
From you to me to you
Opens up our hearts
Rendering the pain askew

Can love change the world
Or was that Lennon's lie
Seeing what it does for us
True love is the perfect high

A Civics Poem

The civil service is all very civil
Your politely made to wait
Whether you're on the outside or not
You will always have to be late

The private sector is all very private
It's quite aggressive too
A power grab for money
It's not an exception, more a rule

The government is all very governing
It's basically contrarianism
With a side salad of pocket lining
Always protected from prison

The journalism is all very journal
The exact definition of which
Is a daily record of news of a personal nature
As it's mostly an opinionated bitch

The arts are all very artistic
Polite, mundane and rambling
The mobile phone has killed aesthetic
No one wants to hear you sing

The classics are o so classic
And will live on in our minds
A kill switch for the brain fog
A product of celestial design

Let's Debate

Let's have a debate
On matters of great importance
Like that crowd have a past
So we can avoid debating rents

And those are ahead of them
If it came to a poll
And those others yet again
Know how to kick the ball

And the substantive issue
The scandal of today
There's really nothing to look at
Another scandal will make it go away

You've never had it so good
Is the newscast we hear
Now we're off for the summer months
To relax with expensive beer

And there won't be talk of NATO
Until at least October
When we'll regain our interest
In Ukraine's misfortune

And we will keep the US companies
That helped Trump and Obama win
Dreaming up the PR
That drowns the bad stuff with a din

Serotonin finds its own level

While I preoccupy
On earth before I die
I find that I strive
To exist and survive

First world problems
Can bring the doldrums
Unhappy is unhappy
As is poverty trappings

And with all the fear
We tend to hold dear
You get in cycles
Of denials and revivals

If a house was free
And the food on the tree
Would we struggle and hate?
If we had a full plate?

I'm not saying I'm poor
But I'm pretty sure
On a whim, my bank
Could make me walk the plank

And I know a few bankers
Around morals, they're dancers
We chase lives of debt
With scoldings to invest

And the point here is?
Is there a true bliss?
I find that I strive
To exist and survive

The Sea

Relentlessly forgiving
Yet at the same time harsh
With brimey silt
And starchy salt

Whilst temperate in Summer
And hard after Autumn
It will wash your soul
And fill your sense

A personal pilgrimage
Every time to Bull Wall
A 'How-do-you-do'
To random bathers

High tide, full moon
Mid morning sun
Here has no currency
Other than the soul

Extradition

Say for example
A Saudi Arabian soldier
Puts a bullet
Through a Yemeni child's head
With a British gun,
Is that a war crime?

Or if indeed
An Isreali troop
Beats a pregnant Palestinian woman
With an iron baton
Outside her own home,
Is that a war crime?

Now let's suppose
An American gun drone
Cruising around Bagdad airspace
Assassinates twenty unarmed men
In five seconds,
Is that a war crime?

Or when a quarter
Of a million civilians
Are murdered in Afghanistan
In a twenty year war
For Western political vanity,
Is that a war crime?

Yet when a man
Exposes all this
Before our eyes
Irrefutably,
How is it viewed?
It is treated as a war crime

Two Way Street

I met a man today on Twitter
Who gave weight to the term trite
Someone had given him an opinion
But the thinking just wasn't quite right

There's a lovely term, 'Contrarian'
Which is what stands for modern Democracy
I say black, he'll say white,
But green is beyond decency

To muster up some outrage
Is a Serotonin drip
Such that the realm of consideration
Is quite particularly thick

But back to this man today,
He weighed heavily on a misguided trope
I could feel the beration
On a salient point I made him note

Convinced that he was right
Based on the fact of self regarding
His concern for our taxes
Was a slanderous asserting of blagarding

Then in from the wings came a Tweeter
Who clarified the lie
Our intrepid hero
Has come to this hill to die

Then silence filled the thread
I suppose he went somewhere else
But no one cared any more
The wall of contrarianism never melts

Maybe that's the lesson
When faced with baseless argument
The truth may always out
At times long after dark

What is it all about?

What is it all about?
Is it a game or a challenge?
The primal survival
Of a homo sapien savage.

The big bang evolutes
To the age of the suit and tie
Yet we always ask
Where do we go when we die?

A PC ain't got a heart

The music industry
is a great big trend
which I mean to say
is mimicry that doesn't end.

It is bland and dry
naive and narcissistic
which I mean to say,
the interest is non existent.

There's no culture
or raw emotion
which I mean to say
they're words with no notion.

The value of a like
is one hundredth of a cent
which I mean to say
no one's going to spend

But it doesn't stop there
this electronic war on art
which I mean to say
a PC ain't got a heart

The Nativity

It's noon and It's wet
On the day we oft forget
That we ever had religion
Or something to imagine

She says Santa isn't real
I guess he's part of the deal
Where youth grows in age
And we turn another page

And here as I think
Of the tenuous link
Between Santa and Jesus
And all the missing pieces

The child is now pleased
She knows not of the ill ease
Of being born in a shed
Of poverty and dread

She doesn't know what to say
I can't tell her either way
She knows what's impossible
I know what's possible

The Local Spar

Sorry bud! Do you have the time?
Yeah it's half past nine
Would you have some change for a hostel?
Sorry no, I haven't got some

Why do you talk of change?
When you are here every day?
You know how it is bud,
There's nothing else to say!

I know what you need,
And you know I know that too.
Yeah but it's not like I'd get a job,
To give me something to do.

Do you not dream of something better?
I dream all the time,
But there isn't anything better
Then the next bottle of wine.

Is there any way I can help
Other than keeping you on the street
With two euros here and there
That keeps you in a heap.

Well there's a general perception
That a beggar is just scum
But every single beggar
Is also a someone

And there's a well held view
That we don't really need help
But those who hold that view don't know
The cards that we're dealt

Don't talk of a place to live
They're only for the rich,
They way I see it though,
They wouldn't survive in a ditch.

Do you want a sandwich in the shop?
That would be great Bud, please!
Tea with milk and sugar?
Four sugars Bud, my hands are starting to freeze!

I buy the sandwich and the tea
And get some change in return
There's nothing else I can really do
Despite my concern

The Eager Programmer

There's a man in my work
and it's fantastic that his presence graces,
because really without him,
we wouldn't be able with our shoe laces.

I'm sure there's many a time,
he has saved us all from calamity,
when treading through the great unknowns
with his immense profundity.

I think I'll donate some wages
to this man in my work,
so he can buy a book on charisma,
because he really is a ....

...eager programmer

Valentines

Is February really the month of love?
When the sea is at it coldest
And it's dark by 6pm
And the people in the street scowl by

As Valentine lays in a chapel across town
Underneath a book of intentions
That has the demeanour of condolences
Signed by touring couples

And romantically we'll have a meal
Both of us will cook
And the children will be at the table
Nintendos setting the mood

No doubt the Hollywood couples
Will be fawning on internet selfies
Marketing their irreconcilable differences
To make poor us look totally unglamorous

But do you know what dear?
As we look to Monday the 14th
I do feel the love
Between you and me

So while it's obviously marketing
And we are both too wise for such
I do believe that truly
Every month is a romantic month

A Junior Cert poem for The Minister for Education

I read today about school books,
and children who didn't have the money,
were sent home with notes,
that really were not very funny,

"If you have difficulty paying this amount in full",
going on to offer instalments
is a very passive aggressive tone
to a parent at the end of their wits.

And I'm thinking back to the hedge schools
where teaching children was against the code
I wonder did those teachers
berate children's parents with a note

But sure we're doing wonders with corporate tax,
and we're winding up the PUP,
now all we need to do,
is make the parents cough up the money.

The Political Debate

Can I please address the panel?
Can I please?
Sorry...
Thank you

I would just like to say,
Sorry, If you don't mind
I would just...
Can I?

I was just going to say,
If I could get a word in edgeways,
If I may...
Please?

I didn't interrupt you,
Will you please let me speak?
You've had your say,
Can I make my point?

Can I just say this,
With all due respect,
The deputy doesn't know what he wants,
It was the same when he was in government

Begging

Have you got a spare cigarette?
Have you got sommit for the ostil?
Sure if you only have a card,
Can you cash back at the cash till?

I'd like to apply for a mortgage,
For thirty years of my life,
Please Mr branch manager,
It's for me and the wife.

Can you let me off the ten cents?
He asked to the shopkeep,
I promise I'll pay you back,
My baby needs this feed.

Can you vote for me,
In the next election?
I promise I'll change the world,
In some unknown direction.

Can I have a pay rise?
I've worked here for years,
Even though I hate this job,
And it brings me to tears.

Can you give me directions,
To get to the main street?
I've been walking, walking, walking.
Now I've concrete feet.

Can you give to this cause?
And that cause and another too?
Christ, where is your conscience?
Is there nothing you can do?

The 1,2,3's

Right Children! We are going to start with the number 1
It's a lonely number and not much fun
After that it doubles to 2
If you have a me, it's great to have a you
Getting on, comes to a 3
The image of you, the image of me
Any more and we have 4
The old biddy next door is keeping a score
Monday to Friday the day ends at 5
Or maybe it starts and you feel alive
By early October it's dark at 6
The little match girl is counting her sticks
On All Saint's Day on the news at 7
They tell us the match girl has gone to heaven
To climb an octave, you need to jump 8
Just make sure you've got some food on your plate
When you're tired, it's bed at 9
Otherwise your mortal coil will draw the line
And at the end, you wind up with 10
Where 1 meets zero and we say 'Amen'

Happiness

What right have you?
To want for any happiness?
Or joy?
Such that the only way to be happy
Is do a line
And pretend it's fun.

Do you need to sell your soul?
to attain anything in this world?
In which case the payback
Will ensure
Sorrow.

The fabricant of religions
All say paradise is beyond
And that we are here in limbo
Until then.

And many sell their souls
For wealth or fame or wisdom
But don't want the other side
Of not owning
Their spirit.

Life is absolutely littered
With hurdle after fence
Where guilt and greed and hope collide
In a war of recompense.

What right have I to happiness?

The Test

I took a COVID test yesterday,
A close contact in the house,
We have to isolate,
And wait for the results to come out.

But is it an imposition?
What is to be our plight?
The missus and I are vaxed,
I'm sure we'll be alright!

We didn't flaunt the regs,
I kept my social distance,
I even gave out on twitter
To the whatabouttery of established musicians.

At lunchtime on the ninth,
We packed in the car to get the test down the road,
And it was all quite pleasant,
Until the medic poked me up the nose.

And now I'm waiting for a text,
And I'm forced to consider life,
One day, my children's mates are around,
The next day, a state of strife.

I don't want to think about dying,
I have a report to finish for three,
It's one thing if you have COVID,
It's quite another for the company.

My nose is a bit runny,
But maybe that's suggestive?
And we all have sore throats,
Are we a COVID collective?

The guidelines say (I think),
It will take two weeks to be free,
Even if we don't have it,
Just then my phone goes ding!

Now there's no more need to rhyme,
We all got the all OK,
We are not going to die,
From my daughter having her friend to play.

9 September 2021

A Gambling (Sorry Charity) Licence

Unaccustomed as I am to public tweeting
I would like to thank all those concerned
The stock exchange index is rising
To talk of inflation is absurd

I would like to thank specifically
All the party advisers
To help us not pay attention
To the accusation of being misers

To all the party canvassers
I wish to extend my thanks
So feel free to let me know
Of any planning applications among the ranks

And now all you party faithful
I'd like to announce the draw
And the winner is our leader's wife
What a coincidence you'll all applaud

(*) This was composed on the occasion of our governing
political party changing the law so that they could operate
under the auspices of a charity to enable them to raise
electioneering monies with expensive raffles.

Decisions

When deciding what to do
About the state of political strife,
Take a leaf from a young person's book
And decide what's worth a fight?

Unfortunately it's not addiction,
Nor is it about the poor.
It's about middle class taxes
To the politician at the door.

If you thought to help refugees,
You really ought know better.
The locals will object strenuously
To politicians in a letter.

Society is bored with the stories,
From schools to hospital beds.
People are anaesthetised
With story after story of dread.

And another windbag steps up
To preach on the late debate
About their sketchy plan
To return everything to great.

And in turn will come an election,
Democracy will be the word.
As children dine in the gutter,
Which the vultures don't find absurd.

And revolution is caged in twitter.
Dissent is a handful of words,
Which the politician don't even read,
When they post to their kindred herds.

So when deciding what to do
About the state of political strife,
Take a leaf from a young person's book
And don't give up the fight!

Incandescence

Incandescent rage on twitter
I'm right, you are wrong
Incandescent rage on twitter
The rebellion is going strong

Incandescent rage on twitter
This hill is where you fall
Incandescent rage on twitter
Opinion from a toilet stall

Incandescent rage on twitter
Everyone can see
Incandescent rage on twitter
Misery begets misery

Incandescent rage on twitter
A bitter competition
Incandescent rage on twitter
Social media or social attrition

Imposter Syndrome

Google describes Imposter Syndrome as
The persistent inability to believe
That one's success is deserved
Or has been legitimately achieved
As a result of one's own efforts or skills.

To put it simply, Imposter Syndrome
Is the experience of feeling like a phoney
You feel as though at any moment
You are going to be found out as a fraud
Like you don't belong where you are
And you only got there through dumb luck.

I watched a linkedin course once
On how to rise to be a manager
And over and over again
This iron pumping bald dude in a shirt and slacks
Gave advice and tuition on being
Unapproachable and elusive to your direct reports.

He would reiterate this mantra
That the ultimate entity was the company
And that if you were in anyway dismissive of this
Then you would need all this american pep talk
That amounted to the opposite of positive affirmation.

There's lots of language in the office
That masquerades as friendly
But only in intonation as really the subtext
Is that you don't fit their match
Implying you are not fit to contribute.

And when all your peers subscribe
To this business model of demeaning
But demeaning in a way that can't be proven in a labour court
You start to wonder
Are they right?
Am I not fit to earn a decent wage?

And the stress comes home
To the kitchen table
Where your middle management middle manager
Is blissfully ignorant of the conversation,
How did your day go today dear?
Not great pet, I was bullied in front of the whole department
again today,
And made turn a two hour task into a two week piece of
useless output.

But this is the society
Our politariat are nurturing
Without even considering
That society is made up of people.
Real people
With real needs
And Imposter Syndrome.

October

There is a certain sense of grief
that comes with October air,
the year is drawing in
and the cold will lay you bare.

The darkness and the grey
casts a shadow in the heart,
and the wind and rain outside
will move the grief to stark.

There is sorrow in the trees
as October removes their coat,
and pours it on the ground.
Ashes to ashes, leaves to muck.

And the general social demeanour
is of sadness and of loss.
The glory of the summer
is gone now, it's lost.

But those reflections of the past
bring a smile to the mind,
when we cast out our nets
at the height of the tide.

I know death will come
as October comes to pass,
but while we are still alive,
our memories will always last.

The Pensioner Poet and the Contents of His Pocket Book

I heard of a man who fought the cause
He wasn't violent but he fought valiantly
With words. Mostly couplets but sometimes obtuse.
Alliterative in his reasoning
He could make the connections
At least in his own head.

Long retired, he would regroup the battalion
At the bar counter every morning
Between Monday and Friday at O-eleven hundred
Sergeant ballpoint and his company of Moleskin pages,
Rations of tea and a will
To win the war.

In his eyes, his thoughts harked at personal epochs
He remembers clearly history as it truly happened
The violence of the past was understood,
Not least because of the futility of oppression
But even because they who reference history
Are blind to its lessons.

Blind. In a way that has no cure,
For while you might learn braille,
There is no assistive aide
To wash away hatred, especially when
It is reinforced with culture
That trains its troops on oppression.

A poet always will return to love
A soldier will continue to leave his love
Whatever the reason might be
And a soldier has no right to deny his violence
When his holy grail is violent
And to be remembered in a poem

So therein is the true conflict.
How to be archived fondly as a killer
By bards who see murder as wrong
As those who pen the soldier's song of death
Write words as base as sewer water
And turn the vehicle of love to threats

By thirteen hundred in the barrack room
The quarter master is changing the kegs
And our erstwhile poet has
Composed another set of peace bidding stanzas.
He trusts completely in the collective conscious
And knows somehow people hear

...the contents of his pocket book.

#Budget23

Poetry is dead
The minister has gone and taxed it
Assonance is at 40 percent
There's no rebate on a couplet

You may have said before
The government is for the birds
It's unlucky that you're hungry
Because there's no nourishment in words

Song is dead too
As all artistic dissent
And we look on incredulous
At the convention of the bent

I'm not angry, I'm not sad
Because I've lived on the street
So you can stuff your extra tenner
But don't think we don't see deceit

Coronation Chicken

We are back to Roman times
My friends
There is no senate and no debate
We all have the bends

And with that comes wars
My friends
There's no peace emissaries
Fight until it ends

Brutus is waiting in the wings
My friends
His knife sharpened to a point
On the message Caesar sends

Augustus is descending the temple steps
My friends
Of, by, for the masses
And the money the rich man spends

The Tiber is a flow of faeces
My friends
The apothecary for the soldier
Is as far as it extends

Think in (Poem for Leo)

Think….
In Metaphors
As if to say your argument
Is terribly clever
And only stupid people wouldn't understand

Like saying
"Inflation is a disease
And we must ease the symptoms
And deal with the underlying causes
Ease the pain", you say

And inflation
Is not Shakespeare
Its mathematics
If people want more profit
They have to take more money

But its companies
Who want more profit
And their org charts
Are Ponzi schemes
Where the board want more profit

But this metaphor
In doctoral economics
It intonations quite factually
That there is no cure
And that its terminal

So your very clever thinking
Betrays you like all drunks
Gratuitously benefacting
The crumbs from our own taxes
And pompous metaphors

The Army

Dear Simon Coveney
I'd like to join your army
I fantasise about murder
And being in a raping party

I don't have any money
And I don't have a roof
But just point me at someone
And I'll shoot the fucking doof

I don't understand politics
And I can't economics
But just give me an Arab
And I'll kick them in the bollocks

I have never had a relationship
With any type of tart
So I think I'm best placed
To ignore matters of the heart

Dear Simon Coveney
Can you send me to NATO
Because I have the IQ
Of a sick blighty potato

What is Progress?

What is progress, I'm left wondering
As I come off social media
In a state of clinical depression
Having hoped for hours to read
Of some success or some positive

But there is no joy in the world
Certainly on the face of it
Nobody seems to want happiness
For anybody else that they don't know
You have to earn it, in money

So if the root of happiness is progress
And the root of progress is ownership
Of your life, of your unborn, of your dreams
And you are told that it will never be
Life cannot be called a game

If there is no happiness
Why are we still fighting to live?
Fighting to live more than others
Why are we killing others
Just so they can kill us back?

And we all hark to be reincarnated
In an infinite Utopia
While we subjugate to the shallow philosophy
That when we go,
That's it, lights out

Nobody lives forever,
At least no one I know,
In a billion years
Our descendants may not have two legs
I suppose that's progress

The Coffee Shop

I don't know why they are called coffee shops
Because really, everyone there drinks tea
Murphy the pensioner wouldn't be at home with an espresso
And Mrs Bourke certainly wouldn't be into the lattes

Now although there is a limited offering of cakes
You wouldn't call it a cake shop either
As we are all very keenly aware
That the croissants would start the day in a bag

There is that European take on the coffee shop
Where Moroccan fragrances, shall we say
Permeate through their customers' patronage
But as I say, not much coffee

I think the metre stick for coffee shops
Was a place in town called Bewleys
Which in fairness, I think was once called a tea rooms
Where serious quantities of tea were processed

Largely because people had nowhere to go
So a fifty pence pot of tea for one
Would last for four hours till the next pot
And would be cold after twenty minutes

All the young ones now, are into their red bulls
And most aren't stuck to while away time as they're still at home
And the tea rooms are now gone
Maybe that's why they are called coffee shops